ANTIGONE

bei
wri
r

Also available by Brendan Kennelly

SOPHOCLES'
ANTIGONE

A NEW VERSION BY
BRENDAN KENNELLY

BLOODAXE BOOKS

Copyright © Brendan Kennelly 1986, 1996

ISBN: 1 85224 363 5 hardback edition
1 85224 364 3 paperback edition

First published 1996 by
Bloodaxe Books Ltd,
P.O. Box 1SN,
Newcastle upon Tyne NE99 1SN.

Bloodaxe Books Ltd acknowledges
the financial assistance of Northern Arts.

Cover printing by J. Thomson Colour Printers Ltd, Glasgow.

Printed in Great Britain by
Bell & Bain Limited, Glasgow, Scotland.

ANTIGONE

Brendan Kennelly's *Antigone* was first performed at the the Peacock Theatre, the Abbey Theatre, Dublin, on 28 April 1986. The cast at the first performance was as follows:

ANTIGONE, *daughter of Oedipus*	Anne Byrne
ISMENE, *daughter of Oedipus*	Pauline McLynn
CHORUS	Peadar Lamb
CREON, *King of Thebes,* *uncle to Antigone & Ismene*	Kevin McHugh
FIRST GUARD, *a sentry*	Séan Campion
HAEMON, *son of Creon*	Darragh Kelly
TIRESIAS, *a seer*	Dónal Farmer
BOY	Seóna Ní Bhriain
SECOND GUARD, *a messenger*	John Olohan
EURYDICE, *Queen of Thebes*	Eileen Colgan
LADY, *attendant on Eurydice*	Maire Ó Neill
ELDERS & GUARDS	Donagh Deeney
	Micheál Ó Briain
	Macdara Ó Fátharta
	Condy Conarain
	Bill Cowley

DIRECTOR	Colm Ó Briain
SET AND COSTUME DESIGN	Bronwen Casson
LIGHTING DESIGN	Leslie Scott
MUSIC COMPOSED BY	Fergus Johnston
SOUND RECORDING	David Nolan
PRODUCTION MANAGER	John Costigan
STAGE DIRECTOR	Bill Hay
STAGE MANAGER	John Kells
ASM	Miriam Kelly
WARDROBE SUPERVISOR	Anne Cave
ASSISTANTS	Rita Sweeney
	Jane MacNally
MAKE-UP	Tony Delany
SET CONSTRUCTED BY	Peter Rose
DESIGN ASSISTANT	Geraldine O'Malley
PROPERTY MASTER	Stephen Molloy

Thanks are also due to Oliver Taplin for help with the cover picture of this Bloodaxe Books edition of Brendan Kennelly's *Antigone*.

ANTIGONE. (*To herself.*) Sickness. Creon. Law. My brothers. Dead.

> (*To* ISMENE.) Sister Ismene, do you know of any sickness,
> Of all the ills spawned by Oedipus,
> That Zeus does not curse us with?
> There's no shame, dishonour, ruin, pain
> Absent from your life and mine.
>
> And now, what do you make of this new edict
> Published by King Creon to all Thebes?
> What is the word? What have you heard?
> Or don't you understand that our friends
> Face the same doomed ends
> As our enemies
> In this city, and all through this land?

ISMENE. Antigone, not a single word of friends,
> Not a single happy or miserable word,
> Has reached me
> Since we two sisters
> Were robbed of our two brothers,
> Killed in a single day.
> Since the Argive host fled
> I might as well be dead
> Because I know nothing more,
> Not, as I have said, one solitary word.

ANTIGONE. I knew it perfectly well.
> That's why I brought you out here,
> Out of that court of sinister stone,
> Where you can hear the word
> All on your own.

ISMENE. What is the word?
> It's clear that you've been
> Brooding a long time on this.
> Antigone, even as a child,
> You were both broody and wild.
> What is the word, I say?

ANTIGONE. Creon has decreed
> That one of our brothers
> Should be buried with honour
> But that the body of the second
> Should be left unburied,

To rot in the heat of the sun,
Be eaten by birds,
Laughed at by men.
Children can throw sticks and stones
At our second brother's naked bones.
Our first brother, Eteocles, it is said,
With proper ritual and dignity
Is laid among the honourable dead.
But the corpse of Polyneices
Must remain unburied,
A thing of shame, unmourned,
A bit of trash
For claws to rip and tear
And beaks to feed on as they will.
Our dead brother's body, all rats and flies,
Must rot in the open air before men's and women's eyes.

That is the word, Ismene. Hear it well.
Brood on the word, dear sister. Action will follow.

Such is the word that Creon the Good
Has laid down for you and for me.
For me, do you realise, for me.
And he is coming here to proclaim the word
To all who do not know it.
Whoever disobeys the word of Creon
Will be stoned to death before the people.
Now that you know the word,
Now that my knowledge is yours, yours mine,
You will soon prove
The nature of your loyalty and love
And whether you are of noble blood
Or the slavish slut
Of a noble line.

ISMENE. If this is what Creon has said
How can I disobey his word
Concerning his treatment of the dead?

ANTIGONE. Brood on this: whether you
Will join with me
In doing what I have to do.

ISMENE. In what you *have* to do?
What do you mean?

8

ANTIGONE. Will you help me
   Bury Polyneices?

ISMENE. Would you bury him
   When such a burial
   Is forbidden by Creon,
   Strongest of men?

ANTIGONE. Polyneices is my brother.
   I can't be false to him.

ISMENE. But Creon's word forbids you.
   Creon's word is law.

ANTIGONE. Polyneices is my brother.
   Creon's word can never change that.
   Creon has no right
   To stop me doing what is right.
   I will do what I believe is right.

ISMENE. Antigone, think how our father died
   Amid scorn and hate,
   His sins forcing him to blind himself
   With his own hand:
   Then his mother and his wife, the same woman,
   One woman with two identities,
   Hanged herself.
   Finally, our two brothers,
   In one day, forged their own doom,
   Each killing the other.
   And now, we two, mere women, are left alone.
   Consider how we will die
   If we disobey the word of Creon.
   Remember this, Antigone:
   You and I were born women.
   We must not go against men.
   I say
   We are ruled by those who are stronger.
   We must obey
   Even when we do not believe
   In our obedience.
   We must obey in spite of disbelief.
   That is my belief. Better to obey and live
   Than disobey and die.
   That is why I will obey Creon.

It is foolish to go against a strong man.
It is foolish to disobey his word.

ANTIGONE. Say what you say, be what you are,
I will bury my brother.
If I am stoned to death
I will be with my brother.
I have more love
For the noble dead
Than for the ambitious living.
I would prefer to live
Among the dead in love
Than among the living in frustration.
Ismene, live as you will.
Dishonour, if you will, those laws
Established in honour by the gods.

ISMENE. I do not dishonour the gods
But I cannot defy the State.
I'm not strong enough for that.
A woman against the State
Is a grain of sand against the sea.

ANTIGONE. I must bury my brother now.

ISMENE. I fear for you, Antigone. How I fear for you.

ANTIGONE. Don't fear for me. Fear your own fear.

ISMENE. At least, tell no one what you plan to do.
Be secret. So will I.

ANTIGONE. Go shout it from the roof-tops, Ismene.
Forget your despicable silence.
Your silence will bring contempt on you
In the end. Be true, not silent.
Tell the blind, servile, murderous world
What Antigone intends to do.
If you're a coward, Ismene, at least be true
To your cowardice. And don't try to turn me
Into a secret version of your cowardly self.

ISMENE. You have a hot heart full of cold words.

ANTIGONE. I know what I have to do.

ISMENE. Do it if you can. But you would
  Try to do what no strong man
  Can do. If a man can't do it,
  How can a woman?

ANTIGONE. When my strength dies, that's when
  I cannot do
  What I must do.

ISMENE. But why attempt a hopeless task?

ANTIGONE. If that is your word, I will hate you
  And so will the dead.
  Leave me with my folly, Ismene.
  To suffer this is nothing
  To the suffering of a shameful death
  Or the pain of a cowardly silence.

ISMENE. Go, if you must,
  But of this be sure:
  Though your task is hopeless
  Those who love you
  Will always hold you dear.
  I love you, my sister.

Enter CHORUS.

CHORUS. The sun itself has saved our land
  Against the proud claims of Polyneices.
  He did his best and worst to destroy us
  But he was beaten back.
  Zeus always hates a boastful man
  And Polyneices was a braggart,
  A vain, arrogant, acquisitive braggart.
  Zeus cooled his proud tongue
  And brought him down to earth.
  A fallen braggart is a sad sight,
  A laughing-stock in the mocking light.

  Zeus saved us from the braggart's tongue and arm,
  From his desire to bring our people harm.
  Zeus brought the braggart low.
  Zeus flipped the coin of battle
  And gave us victory.

And now that we have victory,
Bring on infinite wine.
We'll drink and dance and sing the dark away
Until we stand triumphant in the applauding light of day.

The word is victory for superior men
Who do what they must
While Polyneices corrupts in dust.

But look, here comes Creon, our king,
Our new king because of new fortune
From the gods. Creon is fresh and new
And wise too.
Why has he summoned the wise old men?
What word has he for them?
What word has he for the people?
For all of us who have ears to listen?
What is the word of Creon?

Enter CREON.

CREON. Friends, the State is stable once again
After being threatened by a treacherous man.
I have called you here because I know
How loyal you are to this city, this State.
It is your loyalty that makes us great.
When Oedipus ruled this land, and when he died,
Your loyalty never weakened for a moment.
You are loyal to what is right.
Yours is the proper kind of pride.
Since then, the sons of Oedipus,
The sons of his wife-mother,
The sons of two women in one,
Have killed each other.

Now, I occupy the throne.
My friends, I have come into my own
Because I am close to the dead
And understand the laws they gave to living men.

No man can be known in spirit, mind and soul
Until he understands law and rule.
That is my word to you.
If any leader of the State,
Through fear, keeps his best counsel secret,
I count him a base man.

And if any puts a friend above his country
I count him a man of treachery.
I would not be silent if I saw
My people threatened.
Who can be silent on such matters
If he is loyal to his people?
Who can be silent if he understands the law?
It is the law that keeps our country safe
And if our country's safe, why then we will be friends.
Law is a worker. It works for justice.
Law enables justice to happen as it should, as it must.

That is the rule that will protect this city.
Following that rule, I give you my edict
Concerning the sons of Oedipus:
Eteocles, who died fighting for our city,
Will be buried in full dignity
And rest among the noble dead.
Polyneices, his brother, who came back from exile
And tried to destroy by fire
The city of his fathers
And the shrines of his fathers' gods,
To murder his own brother
And lead our people into slavery,
Polyneices will not be buried.
His corpse will never rest
In the private dignity of the earth.
His corpse must corrupt in the open air,
His corruption must be seen by all, witnessed by all,
Dogs and birds will eat his flesh and bones,
Children throw stones at him for sport,
Shouting his name in mockery,
'Polyneices! Polyneices!
Man of shame! Corpse of shame!'
That will be his special fame.
That is my word.
The wicked are not the just
And must not be treated as if they were.
We have a city to maintain.
It will be maintained by rule, by law,
By men who understand that truth.
These are the men I will honour
In life and in death. My heart is loyal
To loyal hearts.

CHORUS. That is your word, Creon,
    Regarding this city's enemies and friends.
    You have the power to turn your word to action
    For the benefit of all of us,
    Both living and dead.

CREON. Make sure, then, that you guard my word.

CHORUS. Let that be a job for some younger man.

CREON. No, watchers of the corpse have been discovered.

CHORUS. What then do you require?

CREON. That you never take the side of those
    Who break my word.

CHORUS. If a man did that, he'd simply be
    Bringing about his own death.

CREON. That is true; but men have often betrayed
    The truth for money. You are loyal.
    Make sure you never sell your loyalty for money.

Enter GUARD.

GUARD. I give you my word on this –
    I didn't know whether to come quickly or slowly.
    I said to myself 'You eejit, you're
    Going to your doom.'
    And I said to myself 'What, you old slowcoach!
    If Creon hears this from someone else's lips,
    You'll die for it.'
    And so I argued with myself,
    Making a short road long, making that long road
    A road of doubt and pain.
    At last, however, I decided I should come here
    And tell you every word. I would be open and plain.
    The worst that can happen to me is my fate.
    No man can sidestep that.

CREON. What's wrong with you?

GUARD. I want you to hear my own word first:
    I did not do the deed
    Nor did I see who did it
    And yet I want to tell you
    So that no harm will come to me.

CREON. You're a shrewd man
    And know how to protect yourself.
    You obviously have strange words to say,
    Strange news to tell.

GUARD. I have. But bad news is hard to tell.

CREON. Come on, man, out with it.

GUARD. Someone has buried
    The corpse of Polyneices.
    Someone sprinkled dust on the flesh
    And observed the rites that piety demands.
    Whoever did this
    Went away unseen, unheard.
    I give you my word.

CREON. What are you talking about?
    What man alive would dare to do this thing?

GUARD. I don't know.
    There was no sign of spade, shovel or pickaxe.
    The ground was like a rock, unbroken,
    And not a trace of wheels.
    Whoever did it left no hint or sign
    And when the morning-watchman showed it to us,
    A kind of troubled wonder filled us all,
    The wonder at one with the trouble.
    We couldn't see the dead man;
    He wasn't shut in a tomb
    But lightly covered with dust
    As by the hand of someone
    Who wished to shun a curse.
    And there was no sign
    That dog or bird or beast
    Had torn the corpse.

    Then we, the guards, accused each other
    In foul and vicious language.
    We might even have killed each other.
    We were ready to walk through fire,
    To swear to the gods
    That we had nothing to do with it.

    At last, one guard said
    The whole thing must be reported to you.

Not one word must be kept secret –
The whole thing must be told to you.
Only a bad guard would be silent on such a matter.
We drew lots to see who should bring the news.
So here I am, chosen to tell you the story;
I am unwelcome, I am unwilling,
No man wants to the be bearer of bad news.
I bring the truth.

CHORUS. O King, I have been thinking:
Might not this be the work of the gods?

CREON. Quit that foolish talk
Before you drive me mad with rage.
When you say the gods care for this corpse
Your words are foolish, blasphemous, insane.
Why should the gods hide the nakedness of one
Who came to burn their treasures and their shrines,
To flatten their city and destroy its laws?
Why should the gods honour the wicked,
Do homage to the treacherous?
No, not the gods, never the gods!
  From the beginning
There were certain people in this city
Who resented my words
And spoke against me,
Muttering in secret.
They were not content to obey
Like all the people happy with my rule of law.

It is they
Who have bribed others
To commit this crime, this blasphemy.
They have spent money on this crime.
Money is the greatest evil men have known.
Money destroys cities
Maddens men from their homes
Twists decent souls till they
Will do any shameful thing.
Of all evils, money is the King.
It offends the gods
Because money is godlessness.
And it makes a slave,
A dangerous slave, of the man who gives his mind to it.

Whoever did this deed for money
Will pay the price.
And now, I give you my word on this:
If you don't find the man who buried Polyneices
And bring him here before my eyes,
You will be strung up alive
Before you die.
Why?
That you may learn
Not to take money from any source,
Not to sell your soul for money
Not to set your heart on money
Not to blind your eyes with money
Not to spend your days thinking and dreaming of money.
You will find that money
Brings you ruin, not prosperity.

GUARD. May I speak a word? Or should I just leave?

CREON. Even now your words offend me.

GUARD. Are your ears offended, or your soul?

CREON. How would you know where and how I am offended?

GUARD. The deed offends your mind,
My words offend your ears.

CREON. You're just another prattler of this city.

GUARD. Perhaps. But I did not cover
Polyneices with dust.
I am loyal to you. I bring the truth.

CREON. More likely you sold your soul for money.

GUARD. I find it sad
That one who should be a fair-minded judge
Should so misjudge me.

CREON. To hell with all this talk
Of judge and judgment.
If you don't bring to me
Whoever did this deed
You'll find that money
Is the truest source of sorrow.

GUARD. Well, may the culprit be found
          And brought before you for judgment.
          But one thing's sure –
          I'm not so eager to come here again.
          For this,
          I owe the gods great thanks.
          Telling the truth is a dangerous business.

Exeunt.

CHORUS. Wonders are many
          And none is more wonderful than man.
          He possesses the power that outstrips the sea
          Driven by the storm-wind
          Beating the waves that threaten to engulf him.
          He has the power of Earth,
          Eldest of the gods,
          Eternal, untiring,
          Turning the clay with horses and ploughs
          From year to year to year.

          Man, genius, wit, prophet, poet,
          Thinker, worker, sage,
          Controls the hearts of birds in flight,
          The hearts of prowling beasts,
          Beasts roaming the hills.
          He tames the wildest creature,
          Makes him accustomed to the yoke.
          Man is strong and wise and beautiful.

          He tames the mountain bull.

          He tames the wild life of words
          The mad life of thought
          All the dangerous moods
          Of heart and mind.
          He copes with frost and hail and rain.
          He does not flinch from pain.
          Only death defeats him,
          Death, master of the master.

          Baffling even to his own mind
          Is the skill
          Which brings him now to evil,
          Now to good.

18

When he honours the laws of the land
When he upholds the justice loved by the gods,
Secure and proud is his city.
Whoever dishonours the laws of the land,
Scorns the justice loved by the gods,
That man has no city, no right to live in a city,
That man must live where no one lives.
Never may he visit my home,
Never share my thoughts.
That man must know his madness is his own
And is not part of the people, not part of the city.
He is a severed limb,
A severed head, a mad outcast,
Unacceptable to the loyal living
And the restful dead.

Enter GUARD, *leading* ANTIGONE.

What's this?
My soul is stunned.
Antigone?

O luckless daughter of a luckless father –
Oedipus!
What does it mean?
Antigone – a prisoner?
Antigone – breaker of Creon's laws?
Antigone – captured in an act of folly?

GUARD. Here's the girl who did it.
We caught her in the act of burying the corpse.
Where is Creon?

CHORUS. Look, he's coming from the house.
He's needed now.

Enter CREON.

CREON. What's happening here?

GUARD. My King, a man should pledge his word
Against nothing, for later action will belie that word.
Today, I gave my word to myself
I'd never set eyes on you again
Because my soul winced under the lash of your tongue.
But now I have come, bringing this girl
Who was captured as she buried Polyneices.

Here she is. Take her. Question her.
Grill her as you will. But now
I am free, finally, of this trouble.
I told you I am loyal to you.

CREON. This girl – how was she captured?

GUARD. Burying the corpse.

CREON. Do you know what your words mean?

GUARD. I saw her burying the corpse. Your words
Decreed the corpse should not be buried.
Are my words clear? I saw this girl
Burying her brother's corpse.

CREON. Yes, but how was she seen?
How was she captured?
How did all this happen?
Tell me how it happened?

GUARD. When we reached the place where the corpse was,
I could feel the threat of your curses above my head
Beating like the wings of maddened birds
About to swoop and rip my brains and heart out.
I brushed away the dust covering the corpse
And showed again its naked corruption.
Then, with the other guards, I sat down
On the hillside, to windward, in case
I'd be cursed by the stink of that corruption.
Every guard, alert, kept the next man alert
With a fierce stream of threats and curses.
Curses kept us all awake and watchful.

We sat there till the sun began to burn.
Suddenly, a whirlwind wrenched from the land
A storm of dust, blind confusion in the sky,
Darkening the plain, befouling every tree and flower.
I could hear the heavens choking, strangled by the dust.
I closed my eyes, and bore this curse of the gods.

How long that dust raged in its own madness
I'll never know. But when it calmed and dropped,
I saw this girl. She gave a sharp cry
Like a wounded bird or a mother
Brutally stripped of her children.

20

When she saw the corpse deprived
Of the covering dignity of dust,
She cried a cry beyond all bounds of words
And cursed whoever did that deed.
Immediately, she went and got more dust
And once again, began to cover the dead.

      At this point, we rushed forward,
Took her. She offered no resistance.
We accused her of what we'd seen.
She denied nothing, to my joy, to my pain.
To my joy, because I'd escaped your curses.
To my pain, because I had to bring this girl
To judgment. Something about her is so
Noble, so unafraid.
      Yet, to be honest, what matters most to me
Is that I'm safe now.
Safe, although I told the truth.

CREON. You, girl, staring at the earth,
    Do you admit, or do you deny,
    This deed?

ANTIGONE. (*Looking up.*) I admit it, man.

CREON. (*To* GUARD.) Go. You are free.

GUARD *leaves.*

CREON. (*To* ANTIGONE.)
    Did you know my edict had forbidden this?

ANTIGONE. I knew it. It was public knowledge.

CREON. But yet you dared to break the law?

ANTIGONE. Yes. Yours is the word of a man,
    Not of a god. I had to bury my brother.
    I know I must die; that is a grief.
    But to have left a dead brother unburied
    Would have grieved me infinitely more.
    If I seem foolish to you, this may be
    Because you are a foolish man, a foolish judge,
    Spreading your word with foolish law.

CHORUS. This is the daughter of Oedipus.
    She bows before nobody and nothing.
    Her heart is fire. Her mind is ice.

CREON. Yet, there are times when the proudest spirits
  Are most likely to be humbled.
  I've seen the wildest horses tamed by a little curb.
  This girl offers a double insult:
  First, she broke the law;
  Second, now, she boasts of that breaking
  And delights in what she has done.
  A mere girl offers a King a double-insult.
  How will a King endure it?
  How will any man endure it?

  I would be no man,
  She would be the man
  If I let her go unpunished.
  Although she is my sister's child
  She must be punished.
  And so must her sister.
  I charge *her* with conspiracy in this
  Burial of a brother.
  Summon the sister.
  I saw her in the house just now
  Muttering to herself.
  Guilty people mutter much.

ANTIGONE. Would you do more than kill me?

CREON. No.

ANTIGONE. Why do you delay, then?
  Your words repel me.
  My words must be the same to you.
  I sought to bury my brother.
  That is my word, my deed.
  Word and deed are one in me.
  That is my glory.
  And that is what the people think
  And would say
  If they were not afraid of you
  Who have the power
  To say what words you will,
  Do what deeds you will,
  And call it law. Law!

CREON. With these words, you differ
  From all the other people of this city.

22

ANTIGONE. No, my words are theirs, theirs mine,
    But they seal their lips for fear of you
    And the high-and-mighty horror of your law.

CREON. Are you not ashamed to act
    Differently
    From all these other people?

ANTIGONE. No. It is no shame to love a brother.
    It is my love that makes me different.
    It is my difference that you fear.

CREON. Your second brother – did he not die
    For another cause?

ANTIGONE. Brother by the same mother and the same father.

CREON. Why then do you do something hateful,
    Odious, damnable in that other brother's eyes?

ANTIGONE. He's dead and honourably buried.
    How can you know
    What his words might be
    If he stood here before you now?
    Do you presume to know the mind of the dead?

CREON. Would you make the honourable brother
    Equal with the wicked?

ANTIGONE. It was the honourable brother's brother that died –
    Not his slave. His brother, do you understand?
    A brother is a brother anywhere, any time,
    On earth, in heaven, or in hell.

CREON. Yes, but one brother fell
    Attacking the law, the city, the land.
    The other died defending them.

ANTIGONE. Nevertheless, I desire that burial.
    So do the gods.

CREON. In law, which is our sanity and hope,
    The good cannot be treated like the bad.

ANTIGONE. What's evil on this earth,
    May seem blameless in the gods' eyes.
    You may be the King of fools, Creon,
    Though you believe you're wise.

CREON. We must live on this earth.

ANTIGONE. Yet never forget the possible difference
          Of that other world of the gods.
          Thinking of difference there
          May make us different here.
          Creon, you fear the thought of difference.

CREON. An enemy is not a friend,
        Not even in death, or beyond.

ANTIGONE. I have no wish to school myself in hate.
          I want to love.

CREON. Go, then, to your dead, and their difference.
        If you want to love,
        Love your different dead.
        For you, girl, the dead are most real.
        While I live, no woman
        Will tell me how to think and feel;
        Above all, how to rule. I know how to rule.
        That's why I know I am not a fool.

ISMENE *is led in.*

CHORUS. Look, here comes Ismene, crying,
         Like the loving sister she is.

CREON. You're no woman, you're a snake
        Slithering through my house
        Waiting to sting me with your poison.
        How could I know
        That I was nourishing two snakes
        To poison me from my throne
        And make me the sad corpse of a King?
        Now, do you admit
        Your part in this burial?

ISMENE. Yes, I admit my part.

ANTIGONE. No, that is not true.
          You did not agree to the deed.
          You had no part in it
          Nor did I allow you any part in it.

ISMENE. You are in trouble now, my sister.
         I want to be at your side.

24

ANTIGONE. The gods and the dead
    Know it is I
    Who covered the corpse of my brother
    With dust.
    Your words must not belie that fact.
    A sister in mere words
    Is not a sister that I love.

ISMENE. Dearest sister, do not turn me away,
    Nor turn away your head.
    Let me die with you
    And so honour the dead.

ANTIGONE. You will not share my death
    Nor claim to have done something
    Which you have not done.
    My death will do.

ISMENE. My life is nothing without you.

ANTIGONE. Ask Creon; you've got
    Such respect for him.
    You always thought a lot of him.
    You are loyal to his law.

ISMENE. Why do you hurt me, noble blood,
    When it does neither of us any good?

ANTIGONE. If I mock you now, Ismene,
    I mock you out of deepest pain.

ISMENE. Say whatever words you will.
    Let me serve you now with body and soul.

ANTIGONE. You'll serve me best by saving yourself.

ISMENE. Have I, then, no share in your fate,
    Your death.

ANTIGONE. You chose to live for fear.
    I chose to die for love.

ISMENE. At least I made a protest at your choice.

ANTIGONE. There were two worlds, two ways.
    One world approved your way,
    The other, mine.
    You were wise in your way,
    I in mine.

ISMENE. Yet we are both accused
Of the same offence.

ANTIGONE. You will live, my sister, and follow
Your days and nights to their proper end.
My life is an act of service to the dead.

CREON. Look, one of these girls has just shown
How foolish she is. The other
Has been foolish since her days began.

ISMENE. That's how it is, O King.
Nature gives us reason
But there are moments when we squander
Our dearest gifts.

CREON. You squandered the sweet gift of reason
When you chose to die with her.

ISMENE. What is my life without her life?

CREON. Do not speak of her 'life'. That girl is dead.

ISMENE. But will you kill the girl
Who is to marry your own son?

CREON. There are other fish in the sea
Other roads to travel
Other fields to plough.
Antigone was a living woman once. She's dead now.

ISMENE. But never again can there be such love
As bound these two together.
Their two hearts are one.
If Antigone dies, so does your son.

CREON. My son cannot marry one
Who has committed such a crime.
How can an unrepentant, arrogant, blasphemous criminal
Marry my son?

ANTIGONE. Haemon, Haemon, my beloved.
Your father wrongs you deeply now.

CREON. No more words out of you!
No more words about marriage
To my son!

CHORUS. Will you deprive your own son of this girl?

CREON. Death is her husband now.

CHORUS. Creon is determined Antigone must die.

CREON. Yes, I am determined.
    Determined for you, for me,
    Determined for the laws of this land,
    This city,
    Determined for the Kings
    Who will succeed me,
    Determined for today, tomorrow,
    The living, the unborn.
    You know me now. I am determined Creon.
    (*To the* ATTENDANTS.) Take these
    Inside. From now on, treat them
    As women – keep your eye on them.
    Don't give them too much scope.
    Even the boldest woman tries to escape
    When she looks death in the face.
    So hurry, servants, hurry! Take them away!

CHORUS. Blessed are they whose days are free of evil.
    When a house has been cursed by heaven
    It rages from age to age of its people.
    Not a single soul can be forgiven.

    Sorrows of the dead are heaped on sorrows of the living,
    Sorrows of the living heaped on sorrows of the dead.
    Generation cannot be freed by generation
    But each is undeliverable, stricken by some god.

    There is a power no human power can touch,
    There is a law no human law can understand,
    Through the future, as through the past, this law holds good,
    No great force enters mortal life without a curse.

    What comforts some men is deceit to others
    And neither knows if what he feels is true:
    Brothers will love sisters; sisters, brothers,
    And when that love is spent, what will they do?

    A man will think until his mind is fire
    Till good is evil, and evil shines like good;
    A mischievous god may play with his desire
    But who knows how to play with a mischievous god?

Look, Creon,
Here comes Haemon,
The last of your sons.
Is he grieving for the doom
Of his promised bride, Antigone?
How bitter is his heart
For the thwarted hope of his love
Or rather
For his marriage sentenced to death
By his father? Do you dare
Sentence your son's future to death?
Do you dare call yourself his father?

Enter HAEMON.

CREON. We'll soon know the answers to your questions.
Haemon, my son, do you come in rage
Against your father, now that you know
Your bride-to-be is put to death by him?
Or do I have your filial good-will
Whatever I may do? Are you loyal to me,
Loyal and true?

HAEMON. Father, I am your son, and will obey
Whatever the words of your great wisdom say.
What marriage could be a greater gain
Than a father's wise guidance for his son?

CREON. Law governs all happiness,
And this should be your heart's fixed law –
Obey your father's will in everything.
Fathers toil painfully towards their wisdom
But joyfully give that wisdom to their sons.
This is a father's dearest dream –
To see dutiful children grow around him in his home,
To see his children hate his enemies
And love his friends, just as he does himself.
But the man who fathers undutiful children
Makes trouble for himself
And triumph for his enemies.
To ward off chaos, a family must still
Be moulded by the father's will. ·
A father
Is the maker of the future.

And so, my son, do not surrender
Reason to pleasure.
Reason is a king,
Pleasure, a perfumed slut of one night.
Pleasure is sweet weakness,
Reason, stern might.
Pleasure soon grows cold in sweating arms,
You find a treacherous woman shares your bed.
The more treacherous she is, the sweeter are her words.
There's nothing as sweet as treachery.
Now, one true word I have to tell –
This girl will find her true husband in hell.
She has admitted open disobedience.
She sneers at me. No King's voice can still her
Voice. I will not betray my people.
I will kill her.

Let her appeal till she is dead
To the fact that we are kindred.
Disobedience is the worst of evils –
It destroys cities
Maddens men from their homes
Twists decent souls till they
Will do any shameful thing.
Of all evils, disobedience is the King.
It offends the gods
Because disobedience is godlessness.
Obedience is the key to fairer living.
Therefore, we must not allow
A disobedient woman
To tear us apart.
If I must fall from power
Let it be by a man's hand,
Never by a woman's.

CHORUS. Creon, your words seem wise.

HAEMON. Father, the gods have given us the sweet gift of reason,
  The most humane and priceless of all their gifts to men.
  I lack the skill to say where your words are wrong
  And yet another man may have a helpful thought.
  For your sake, I listen to what all men say,
  Your dreaded frown does not encourage people to be
  Truthful. But I have heard them muttering in dark places

Concerning this girl, such words
As would offend your ear:
  'Why should such a girl,
Who did such a noble thing,
Meet such a shameful death?
When her brother died in battle
She would not let him be unburied
To be devoured by beasts and birds and dogs
But shrouded him in the dignity of dust.
Far from deserving death,
Does not this girl
Deserve every golden honour
The State can offer?'

Such are the words that circulate in secret.
Father, nothing matters to me like your welfare.
I want you always to prosper.
Do not persist, then, in one mood alone.
The world is full of different words, different voices.
Listen to the words, the voices.
Do not be a prisoner in yourself
Although you are a King of others.
For if any man thinks that he alone is wise,
Then, my father, he's in danger of being mad.

I beg you, permit yourself to change,
Do not embrace the madness of being fixed
Forever in yourself. If you love your people,
You will listen to them. If you listen
To your subjects, you will be a greater King.
The only object of a great King
Is to be greater still.
So listen well.

CHORUS. Father, listen to your son.
  Son, listen to your father.
  Learn from each other.

CREON. Is a man of my age and experience
  To learn from a boy of his limited sense?

HAEMON. I say nothing that is not right
  Insofar as I understand what is right.
  If I am young, consider my sense,
  Not my years.

CREON. How can I honour disobedience?

HAEMON. I do not wish you to show respect
For anyone who does wrong.

CREON. (*Furious.*) She has done wrong.
She knows she has done wrong.

HAEMON. (*Calmly.*) The people say that she has done no wrong.

CREON. Shall the people tell me how to rule?

HAEMON. Listen to the people, for now you speak
Like an inexperienced boy.

CREON. This is my land. This land I have to rule.
Must I listen to the voice of every fool?

HAEMON. No man can rule alone.
No single city belongs to any single man.

CREON. Is not the city the creation
Of the ruler's vision?

HAEMON. You'd make a good King of the desert.
The sand would never disagree with you.
Neither would the rats.

CREON. You speak for women.
You speak for this girl.

HAEMON. If you are a woman
My love is for you.
I work for your good fortune.
That is my word, father. My word is true.

CREON. Are you mocking me?
Are you openly defying me?

Haemon. No, I tell you you do not listen.
Why do you not listen to me?
Why do you not listen to your people?
What else is justice
But listening to the voices of the people
And then, with the help of the gods,
Deciding what is right?
Father, you offend justice.

CREON. How do I offend justice
When I respect my own judgment?

HAEMON. You do not respect justice
　　When you trample on the voices of the people.

CREON. You do not mean the people.
　　You mean woman.
　　You would put a man below a woman.

HAEMON. Insofar as I understand
　　What is happening here,
　　I try to be fair.

CREON. You are pleading for that girl.

HAEMON. I plead for her
　　For you
　　For me
　　And for the gods above and below,
　　The gods who whisper in my heart.

CREON. You will never marry her now.

HAEMON. Then she must die, and by her death
　　Destroy another.

CREON. You dare to threaten me?

HAEMON. What threat is there
　　In fighting such stupidity?

CREON. You'll regret this.

HAEMON. You'll regret your speaking of regret.

CREON. You sad little boy, you woman's slave,
　　Out of my way.
　　Go, be a woman
　　Since you understand the thing so well,
　　Be a woman like the woman
　　Whose brother was condemned to rot in public hell.

HAEMON. You would speak
　　But not let me speak?

CREON. Now, by the gods, hear my word.
　　You shall suffer for making me
　　Suffer your mocking disobedience.
　　Bring forth that girl,
　　That hated thing, to die
　　Here, now, before his eyes,
　　The criminal bride at the mocking bridegroom's side.

HAEMON. No, never at my side shall Antigone die.
　　　Never again shall you look upon my face.
　　　Rave and rage as best you can
　　　Among the friends who still consider you a man.
　　　You have your loyal friends, my father.
　　　They tell you all the lies you want to hear.

Exit.

CHORUS. Your son is gone.
　　　The man is gone, O King,
　　　In angry haste.
　　　A pure and youthful mind, when hurt,
　　　Can lay the world to waste.

CREON. He is no man. My son is not a man.
　　　So let him do or dream what he can.
　　　He'll not save these two girls
　　　From their doom.

CHORUS. Are you going to kill them both?

CREON. No. Thank you for that just thought.
　　　I wish to be just, I wish to be fair.
　　　I will not kill that girl
　　　Whose hands are pure.
　　　Thank you for that question.
　　　Your question has saved her life.

CHORUS. And how will you kill Antigone?

CREON. I will take her to the loneliest place in the world.
　　　It is a hole among the rocks,
　　　A black pit of emptiness.
　　　I will give her food,
　　　But she must live forever
　　　In that dark hole, blacker than any midnight.
　　　There, let her do as she will –
　　　Pray to the gods, they may rescue her
　　　If they are able.
　　　I want Antigone to think of her life
　　　As she lies in that black hole
　　　Among the rocks,
　　　Why she broke my law,
　　　Why she did not believe each word
　　　That in all sincerity I said;

Why, above all, she mocks the lawful living
And gives her love
To the shameful dead.
I want Antigone to think,
To think until she knows
In every corner of her being
Why she wasted her life
For nothing.

Exit.

CHORUS. Love, you are the object of our lives,
    Love, you are the truest crime;
    Love, you prove the obscenity of money,
    Love, you are a waste of time.

    Love, you live in the heart of a girl,
    Love, you are the spittle on an old man's lips,
    Love, you are a suburban nightmare,
    The soiled lace-curtains from which a heart escapes.

    Love, you help a child to grow up,
    Love, you fill the eyes of a young bride;
    Whatever they say of you, O love,
    You're always dying, yet never completely dead.

ANTIGONE *is led out to her execution.*

    Now, I move beyond the bounds of loyalty,
    All Kings I scorn, for Antigone I cry,
    Antigone, passing to the darkness
    Where she must die, Antigone
    Whose fiery heart would never let her tell a lie.

ANTIGONE. I go on my last journey,
    Looking my last on the sunlight.
    Because I have given my life to the dead
    I have never stretched in the marriage-bed.
    I'll never know the thrust of living blood,
    The Lord of the Dark Lake I shall wed.

CHORUS. You go to the dead,
    Without plague or sickness on your head.
    You have chosen and shaped your own fate
    Unlike these women
    Who have to prowl among men

Or other women
For their little pleasures.
You have created your own solitude.

ANTIGONE. I am afraid of my fate,
As if it were something
That might choke me
Like a chicken-bone
Stuck in my throat.
Why do I think of eternity
As choking me
Like ivy choking a house?
My hands leap to cover my eyes.

CHORUS. Your hands at your eyes!
So it was with many a goddess.
And, like many a goddess,
You must keep your hands before your eyes.

ANTIGONE. Mock me, if you will.
I do not doubt that you are able.
You are used to flattering men.
But I am a woman
And must go my way alone.
You know all about men,
You know all about power,
You know all about money.

But you know nothing of women.

What man
Knows anything of woman?

If he did
He would change from being a man
As men recognise a man.

If I lived,
I could change all the men of the world.

I go to live in a hole in the rocks.
Think of me there.

I am a woman without fear
In a hole in the rocks
Where no man or woman dare venture.

CHORUS. You have gone to the utmost edge of daring
    And you have fallen.

    Is this because of your father's sin,
    Old horny Oedipus? He knew two women in one.
    Is this his legacy to you? A hole in the rocks. Black hole.
    Alone.

ANTIGONE. You have touched my deepest fear.
    You have opened my father's head.
    You have looked into my mother's bed.
    You know why I have given my life
    To the unburied dead.

    And now I go to them.

    I go to my father, foolish boy,
        foolish lover, foolish man.

    I go to my mother, kind soul,
        foolish woman.

    I go to my brother whose corpse
        I sprinkled with dust.

    I go to the gods, the gods' beds,
        the gods' lust.

    O my loving brother, my love for you
    Has robbed me of my life.

CHORUS. Antigone, you have destroyed yourself.

ANTIGONE. I go alone.
    Let no one weep for me.
    Let no friend think of me.
    I never knew a man
    Or heard his worlds upon a wedding-night.
    I walk a cold road to my death.
    It's no use now
    Looking back
    Or looking forward.
    I go alone.

Enter CREON.

CREON. Take her away!
When you have placed her
In that black hole among the rocks,
Leave her there, alone.
Banished from the world of men,
This girl will never see the light again.

ANTIGONE. That black hole among the rocks
Will be my prison
Bridal-chamber
Tomb.
From there I go to my father,
My mother and my brother.
My brother! It is for you I suffer this.
This is my reward for loving you.
And yet I only gave you what was rightly yours.
If I had been the mother of children,
If I had a husband in my home,
I would not have done for them
What I did for you.
Why do I speak such words?
A lost child can be replaced
And other husbands can be found.
But when my father and mother are dead
No brother's life
Can ever flower in me again.
In me flourished the very best of men.
Men!
Creon!
He sends me to my grave
Because I acted out my love.
I never knew the marriage-bed
I heard no bridal song
I knew no happy married love
No joy of children.

What law have I broken?
My crime was love.
Loving my brother was my sin.
That is the law of man.

CHORUS. The girl is torn in all directions!

CREON. Let these damned guards be quick.
Take her away.

ANTIGONE. These words are stones
  Battering me to death.

CREON. You have no hope, girl.
  You are going to die.

ANTIGONE. Men are leading me to death.
  Men made the law that said I'm guilty.
  Men will place me
  In a black hole among the rocks.
  Men will deny me light.
  Yet all I did was for a man
  Whom other men called evil.
  Because I would not kill my love,
  My love kills me.
  In this place, killers of love go free.

ANTIGONE *is led away.*

CHORUS. Imagine! A daughter stuck in a black hole,
  Buried alive in a hideous pit
  Among the rocks!

  A daughter!

  She is the light of life
  The better part of a man's blood
  The transformation of crude manhood
  Into a creature to be loved by men
  She is the reason for his being
  She opens him up to himself
  Through her he may know himself
  And know more deeply the proud pain of love

  A black hole among the rocks
  No light
  No light

  Buried alive

  Victim of love
  Victim of law

  Daughter in the darkness

  Blind to the world of men

Enter TIRESIAS, *led by a boy.*

TIRESIAS. Creon, it takes a boy
  To lead an old blind man
  Into your presence.

CREON. Tiresias, what brings you here?

TIRESIAS. Listen to my words.

CREON. I have listened to them before.

TIRESIAS. Yes; and when you listened,
  Things worked well for you
  And for your city.

CREON. That is true.

TIRESIAS. Listen, Creon. There is a knife at your throat.

CREON. What – what do you mean?

TIRESIAS. I sat in the light, listening
  To the wings of birds.
  The birds were mad with rage.
  As they ripped each other in the air
  I listened to the voices of their wings.
  I heard what the voices said.

  In fear, I offered sacrifice
  But I could make no fire.
  Instead, the flesh oozed from the bones.

  The bones were naked in the sun.

  I asked this boy to tell me what was wrong.
  I listened to the boy. The boy had listened to men and women.
  I know now that you have poisoned this city
  By refusing burial to the corpse of Polyneices.
  The gods refuse all sacrifice and prayer
  And the birds of the air are mad
  Because they have eaten the flesh
  And tasted the blood
  Of the rotting corpse
  Of the son of Oedipus.

  Listen to me, Creon.
  Think of my words, and act on them.
  Bury that corpse.

CREON. You are an old man.
    You see things.
    We agree you are a seer.
    Seeing is your trade.
    For all your seeing in the past, you were well paid.
    Take money where you will
    But do not tell me
    What to do with that corpse
    Just because someone has given you money.

TIRESIAS. Who knows what – ?

CREON. What are you saying?

TIRESIAS. Who knows what truth is in the words of those
    Who come to you, offering
    The wisdom of their hearts and minds?
    Are you prepared to listen to good words?

CREON. Yes, but not to foolish talk.

TIRESIAS. You are foolish, Creon.

CREON. I'll let that insult pass.
    I'll not insult you, Tiresias.

TIRESIAS. You *do* insult me, when you say
    My words are foolish.

CREON. Seers and prophets
    Always had a weakness for money.

TIRESIAS. And the children of tyrants
    Always corrupted the State.

CREON. Do you know, old man,
    You are speaking to your King?

TIRESIAS. I know it well: for by my words
    You saved this city.

CREON. I approve your wisdom
    But not your love of evil men,
    Not your love of the corpse.

TIRESIAS. Would you make me speak the words
    That create dread in my soul?

CREON. Speak your words – but not for money.

TIRESIAS. No hope of that from you.

CREON. Speak!

TIRESIAS. One of your own blood will be a corpse soon
    Because you have condemned to darkness
    A daughter of light
    And because you have left unburied
    One who belongs to the gods.
    You have violated a law
    And continue to do so.
    That is why you will be punished.

    In a short time
    There will be wailing in your house.
    All the cities of this land
    Throb with hatred for you
    Because dog and bird and beast
    Carry the pollution of the unburied corpse
    Through all their streets
    Until it fills their houses
    Reeks at their tables
    Infects their children
    And poisons the very bed of love.

    You asked for my words.
    You have them now
    And every word is true.
    Creon, the birds of the air have told me
    That you spread evil everywhere.

    Boy, lead me to my home
    And let this ignorant King
    Meddle with younger men.
    Let him learn to keep
    A temperate tongue in his head.
    Let him learn respect
    For the living and the dead.
    Let him think
    All day, all night
    Until he begins to suspect
    He may not be always right.

Exeunt.

CHORUS. Tiresias has spoken cutting words
    And his voice is always true.

CREON. His words trouble my soul.
    But how can I give in now?
    Yet not to surrender
    May bring destruction.

CHORUS. Listen to my words.

CREON. Speak.

CHORUS. Release the girl.
    Bury the corpse.

CREON. Is this your word to me –
    That I surrender?

CHORUS. Yes, and quickly too.

CREON. Quickly? This is monstrous.
    And yet if I – if I do not –
    Yes, yes, I must obey.
    I must change my mind.

CHORUS. Free the girl yourself.
    Bury the corpse yourself.
    Do not wait for others.

CREON. Yes, I'll go as I am.
    I'll free the girl
    And bury her brother's corpse.
    But why now, even now, do I break
    My own law? Why do I break the law
    That all my life I worked and struggled to uphold
    For the good of my people? My own people?

CHORUS. A change of mind, a change of heart
    Allows the gods to play their part.
    If the change take place in a stubborn King
    Is there hope of further blessing
    Breathing from the stars' deep fires
    New words to rectify old mad desires?
    Is the change of heart in time?
    Or too late?
    Whose in the law? Whose is the crime?

I send my words like birds into the sky
Turning to black dust in a cloud of anarchy,
Nightmare of law, perfect folly of human art,
You see and witness all, god of the change of heart.

We fix and label you with whatever names we will
You smile at every name's bewildering syllables,
The ease with which the dead rip the living apart,
Bread upon your table, god of the change of heart.

Fixed mountain, restless river suggest the family is good,
Law and ritual would cage the demons in the blood,
What must a King do, if his son is a rebel upstart?
Your lightest mood may shock the land, god of the change
        of heart.

To persist in one conviction is to set teeth against a stone,
To believe in one thing only is to live with a word alone,
A man burns others with his words, choosing his special mark;
Pity that triumphant man, god of the change of heart.

Your toy is time, your child is man, he plays on the world's
        floor,
Loving, judging, cursing, erring – but always wanting more;
And more he gets, and more he gets, while you sit still, apart;
Turn horror to delight
Suffering to song
Misery to joy
Hatred to love
Curses to blessings

But will the mind see in time

God of the change of heart?

Enter MESSENGER.

MESSENGER. Creon saved our land
        And was once a blessed man.
        Justice sweetened his every word.
        Then he changed
        And became like a living corpse,
        All the joy
        Drained from his soul.
        And now he must face new grief.

CHORUS. What grief?

MESSENGER. His son is dead. Haemon is dead.

CHORUS. How?

MESSENGER. By his own hand,
    In hate and rage at his father.

CHORUS. Tiresias, your words are true!
    Here is Creon's wife, Eurydice.

Enter EURYDICE *and her* ATTENDANT.

ATTENDANT. My Lady, why are you so distressed?
    You should have returned to rest
    In your own house.
    As you were passing through the gate
    You stopped, as if stricken,
    And muttered something about words
    That knew no mercy.
    Wherever they came from,
    Whatever they said,
    They stole the wholesome colour from your face
    And turned your living beauty
    Into the very picture of death.
    And yet, it is not too late for you to rest.
    Your mind will find sweet peace again
    Because your heart is blessed.
    Let these merciless words
    Fly out of your heart like lunatic birds
    Into the indifferent skies,
    Rip each other to pieces
    Where no human eyes
    Can see their madness rage
    In wing and beak and claw,
    No human ears
    Hear their lost, last cries.
    Dear lady, speak to me
    As you have spoken to me all these years.
    What words did you hear?
    Why did you grow pale and tremble
    As though with some unbearable fear?
    Why did your body shake in terror
    When your hand rested on your own familiar gate?

Look at me, dear lady, I am here
As I have always been here.
Here.
Why do you stare
As though the only purpose of your life
Is to make a clear word
Doubly clear?

EURYDICE. (*Staring at her* MESSENGER.)
I heard these words as I was going to pray.
My heart became a place of prayer,
Happy to speak out of its own silence
To the listening silence of my god.
But the words that shaped my prayer
Were strangled by your words of murder.

(*She moves towards the* MESSENGER.)

Murder! Do you hear me? Murder,
Although you did not use that word.
I heard everything you said
But my heart, my mind, my blood
Will not believe my son is dead.
Dead! How can my son be dead?
You speak as if from another country,
A land of more-than-human grief.
Between us
Is a sea of disbelief.
I am drowning in that sea.
No prayer that I have said,
Or hoped to say, or dreamed but left unsaid,
Can lighten my heart now.
Death and disbelief are the air I breathe today,
This killing air, merciless and raw.
And yet I know I must believe
What is.
Not to believe what is
Would bring worse pain
If such can be imagined.
Your words of cruel truth are now my only law.
Your words! I will hear your words again.
Come near! Come near! Tell me what you saw.

MESSENGER. Dear lady, I will tell you what I saw.
I went with Creon to where the corpse lay.
We washed it
And raised a mound of his native earth.
We turned, then, to free the girl
From that black hole in the rocks.
I heard this crying from that place
And hurried with Creon there.

As the King approached,
He seemed clothed in those cries.
He groaned in pain and said
'I hear my son.' Again: 'I hear my son.'

I went in among the rocks.
I saw Antigone hanging by the neck.
I saw Haemon
With his hands around her waist,
Crying of his lost love
And in the same breath
Cursing his father.
The words of love mixed fearfully with the words of cursing
In that hole among the rocks.

Creon begged his son
To come into the light
But the boy glared at him
With maddened eyes
And tried to kill his father
With his great cross-hilted sword.
He missed his aim.
And then he leaned his body on the sword
And drove it through himself.
With his last breath
He embraced Antigone.
Then it was corpse embracing corpse
In the black hole of death.

Exit EURYDICE.

CHORUS. Why has Eurydice left without a word?

MESSENGER. I don't know. Perhaps to grieve in private.
I'll go into the house and find out.

Exit.

Enter CREON *with* ATTENDANTS *bearing the body of* HAEMON.

CREON. My son, dead by his own hand,
　　　But more by stubborn and killing words:
　　　My son.

CHORUS. Is the change of heart in time?
　　　Too late. Witness the crime.

CREON. What made me so cruel?
　　　What made my heart
　　　So stubborn and hard?
　　　Why was I so cruel and blind,
　　　An upright corpse of cruelty?

Enter MESSENGER.

MESSENGER. Your queen is dead.

CREON. Mercy!
　　　Is there no mercy in the world?
　　　I am a dead man.
　　　Eurydice, my dear, dear wife –
　　　Dead. All dead.

MESSENGER. She stabbed herself
　　　And died heaping curses on your head.

CREON. Is there anyone to kill me?

MESSENGER. With her dying breath
　　　Eurydice blamed you
　　　For the deaths of Haemon and Antigone.

CREON. Eurydice – she killed herself?

MESSENGER. Yes, as I have said.

CREON. Your word is wrong.
　　　I killed Eurydice.
　　　Whatever future waits me now
　　　Is only days and nights of guilt.
　　　I live to pollute the world.
　　　Let me die, please, please, let me die.

CHORUS. There is a future,
　　　You must cope with that.
　　　There is a present,
　　　We all must cope with that.

There are so many things to do
In this land, this city.

CREON. Not long ago, that thought
Was a good dream filling all my life.

CHORUS. Dream no more.
Live with what you are.

CREON. What am I?
A foolish man –
I killed my son
I killed my son's love
I killed my wife
I killed my happy self.
Wherever I look now
I see accusing ghosts,
I hear only
The accusing words of the dead.
Why did I not listen to the words of the living?
Why did I not listen?

Exit.

CHORUS. To be wise is to be almost happy.
The god's laws
Are the laws we must observe.
Our little strength is nothing
Set against their might
And the ringing words of proud men
Are children's frightened whispers in the night.

ANTIGONE

Endnotes by
BRENDAN KENNELLY
TERENCE BROWN
KATHLEEN McCRACKEN

BRENDAN KENNELLY
Doing Justice to Antigone

While writing *Antigone* I noticed that the characters seemed to come more and more alive with each re-writing as if, in this play where people are constantly judging others and being in turn constantly judged, they wish themselves and what they believe and do to be properly understood, to be accurately evaluated, to have justice done to them. Justice is of paramount importance in *Antigone*: and it is frequently in conflict with reality. I would define justice as a vision of what *should* prevail; reality I would define as the knowledge of what *does* prevail. Antigone is in the grip of her vision of justice and she wants to make it reality. Creon, too, is in the grip of his vision and he is determined to make it prevail. But Antigone's vision of justice, love and loyalty is not Creon's.

We have a conflict of visions, a conflict of two passionate people, two living hearts, brought about, perhaps ironically, by the dead Polyneices, or rather by attitudes among the living to the burial or non-burial of his corpse. Behind these conflicting attitudes are a number of histories: histories of family relationships, of personal values, of civil stability, of political change, of the growth of power and effective government, of ideas concerning what actually constitutes civilised living. These histories are like insistent, vigorous ghosts haunting every word that the characters say. This is a truly haunted play; the presence of the dead in the hearts and minds of the living is a fierce, driving and endlessly powerful force. This presence haunts the language and makes it, at certain moments, tremble with a peculiar intensity.

At the end, one is left with more questions than answers. What is the deepest source of Antigone's passion? What was Polyneices like? Why does Antigone feel with such unquestioning and unquestionable intensity about him? Are love and loyalty one and the same? What is Creon's concept of loyalty? What is Ismene's? What is Tiresias's? Haemon's? What is the influence of the dead on the living? I'm sure there are many people today who would reply – very little influence, very little indeed. But there are others who would reply in a very different vein. This version of *Antigone* tries to be true, to be loyal to my understanding of the Greek world; but it must also be loyal to my experience of life in Ireland, in the modern world. We are all both limited and stimulated by such experience. Family life. Brothers and sisters. Fathers and mothers. Moments of love and hate. Public life. Governments. Politicians. Rulers. People making speeches. People interested in power. People whose hearts and minds are moulded by power. People who betray, conspire and manipulate in order to achieve power.

So in any serious, sustained attempt to "translate" a play like *Antigone*, the conflict between past and present in the mind of the translator is as real as any conflict in the play itself. We are all, to some extent, creatures of conflict and, when we come to use words, we struggle to be true to our experience and understanding of that conflict. Conflict is served by the language it creates.

The ancient, original Greek infiltrates life in modern Ireland. In many ways, the past shapes and directs the present. The past educates and enlightens the present. The present selects from that education, that enlightenment, and makes its own way forward, as we all must, into a future that can be known only by experiencing it, and then only partially, depending on our willingness to give ourselves with whatever passion we are capable of into the arms of every moment that is waiting to be lived.

Antigone lives with passion because of her loyalty to, and love for the dead. But in living out her love for her dead brother she loses her love for Haemon, her living lover, Creon's son. There is a conflict between the claim of a dead brother and a living lover. This conflict is resolved 'in a black hole among the rocks'. Or is it? Will the consequences of what happens in that 'black hole' resonate among the unborn, the Antigones, Creons and Haemons of the future? The present is soon the past. The future becomes the present. The mills of consequence grind on.

Even now, after many re-writings, the more I think about this play the more questions present themselves. That fact is, perhaps, the truest testimony to the strange complexity and enduring attraction of *Antigone*.

February 1996

TERENCE BROWN
An Uncompromising Female Spirit

Oedipus King of Thebes is dead. His two sons Eteocles and Poly-
neices have fought a fratricidal war for the succession which has
left them both dead too. Creon is now king and has issued an
order that whereas Eteocles can be buried with all appropriate ob-
sequies, Polyneices' corpse must be left to rot – prey to bird, beast
and dog. The protector of the city will be honoured, the rebellious
exile must suffer opprobrium even in death: 'The wicked are not
the just/And must not be treated as if they are'. Oedipus's daugh-
ter Antigone will have none of such politic judgement. The ancient
pieties must be observed, even on pain of death. So she acts. Per-
forms ritual service for her kin. So tragic devastation is wrought
upon a doomed household.

This starkly simple plot which the Western imagination has in-
herited from fifth-century Athens (the plot may indeed originate
with Sophocles' text) has had a recurrent life in the very many
versions of it which poet and dramatist have attempted in modern
times. It has been in periods of particular civil and political strife
that it has most profoundly appealed. The early 19th century for
example, in the wake of the French Revolution and the Napoleonic
imperium, canonised Antigone as sacrificial victim, proto-Christ. Her
death spoke of the crushing of aspirations to sexual and personal
liberation that the revolution had unleashed. And it was during the
Nazi occupation of Paris that one of this century's most resonantly
political Antigones came to life in Anouilh's version.

The conflict which this play dramatises, between *real-politik* and
unyielding principle, between the social requirement that order be
maintained and the absolute demands of ancestral piety is a con-
flict made painfully real in many of the crises that have challenged
this nation in the recent past. That such conflict is symbolised in
a battle of wills between a powerful man and a vulnerable but in-
domitable young woman must have peculiar significance for a soc-
iety undergoing a protracted and often fraught adjustment of its
fundamental attitudes to sexuality. It touches some of our deepest
anxieties, echoes our intimated hopes.

Brendan Kennelly's version of the *Antigone* is absorbed by two
things: the mysterious gulf between words and deeds and the claus-
trophobic intimacy of family life. The first of these finds expression

in the work's admiration for an Antigone for whom word and deed are one. The second is expressed in the play's stark highlighting of the terms of familial and sexual relationship – brother, sister, child, father, daughter, husband, wife, boy, son, girl, woman, man. It is as 'man' that Antigone chooses to address King Creon at her moment of pure rebellion. An uncompromising female spirit declares itself in radical opposition to Creon's male authority.

A poet's fascination with a figure in whom word and deed are one is what links the author of this version to those 19th century romantics who found in Antigone a symbol of a total integrity of being, who saw in her a sacrificial victim, a scapegoat. That Brendan Kennelly also re-creates the legendary plot as a family romance, as a domestic tragedy whose victim is Creon as well as Antigone tells us that the 20th century must experience this Sophoclean drama in the light of lessons derived from another of the master's works, the tragedy of King Oedipus.

April 1986
Reprinted from the Peacock Theatre programme for *Antigone*.

KATHLEEN McCRACKEN
Site of Recovery: Brendan Kennelly's *Antigone*

Brendan Kennelly has written versions of four classic plays: Soph-
ocles' *Antigone*, Euripides' *Medea* and *The Trojan Women*, and Lorca's
Blood Wedding. All four allow for the extension of themes and tech-
niques present in his earlier writing and pose challenges which are
valuable to Kennelly both in his development as a writer and in
terms of the issues he would put to a contemporary Irish audience.
Indeed, he follows an established practice among modern and con-
temporary Irish poets. From Yeats's *King Oedipus* and *Oedipus at
Colonus* and MacNeice's *Agamemnon* through to the spate of recent
versions (including Tom Paulin's *The Riot Act* and *Seize the Fire*,
Aidan Carl Mathews' *Antigone*, Seamus Heaney's *The Cure at Troy*,
Desmond Egan's *Medea* and Derek Mahon's *The Bacchae*), the
technical challenge of translating, adapting or, as has more often
been the case, transposing or interpreting classical Greek dramatic
texts has been bound up with the impulse not just to create 'para-
bles for our times' but also with a need to re-examine precisely
those binary oppositions and 'specific universals' which George
Steiner, in his seminal study of the Antigone myth, identifies: 'the
confrontation of justice and law, of the aura of the dead and the
claims of the living...the hungry dreams of the young [and] the
"realism" of the ageing'.[1]

Although a comprehensive study of the connections between
these Irish versions has yet to be made, Anthony Roche's essay
'Ireland's *Antigones*: Tragedy North and South'[2] gives a detailed
analysis of four versions of *Antigone* scripted in 1984: Paulin's *The
Riot Act*, Mathews' *Antigone*, Kennelly's *Antigone* and Pat Murphy's
film *Anne Devlin*. Roche finds Kennelly's version 'the least obvi-
ously Hibernicised' in terms of idiom and political metaphor, and
certainly if we were to place Kennelly's versions alongside those
of his contemporaries his would appear comparatively apolitical. If
Kennelly's version of *Antigone* is less overtly political, if it is more
conservative in its interpretation of the original text, this is in part
because his interest lies not so much in Paulin's parabolising of
certain figures and events in Irish and Northern Irish politics, or in
Mathews' experimentation with postmodernist stagecraft (though
both tactics are to some degree implicit in his project) as in stress-
ing the feminist imperatives and, by extension, the broad human-

ist ramifications, which emerge naturally out of Sophocles' play. Roche proffers an astute feminist reading of the play, and, of the three male-authored versions he considers, concludes that Kennelly's pushes furthest in this direction, but that it too falls short of being a 'truly feminist Antigone'. 'Having brought us to the edge, Kennelly can go no further, both because his literary source does not and because that "black hole" is a woman-centred space towards which none of the three male writers…can do more than gesture'.[3] Since *Antigone*, Kennelly has gone well beyond this point. In the three plays which have followed he has moved progressively further into that 'woman-centred space' which, almost a decade ago, may well have seemed off-limits. Consequently we are able to reconsider Kennelly's *Antigone* both in its own right and as the foundation for his move into drama.

The signal issue debated in Kennelly's *Antigone* is well-defined by one of his literary touchstones, Blake's dictum 'True progress is possible only between opposites'.[4] Kennelly's belief that Ireland's difficulties are rooted in the failure of 'closed minds' to embrace that which is other and opposite, whether in terms of historical reality, political and religious affiliation, gender or nationality, is concretised in the clash between the play's protagonists, Antigone and Creon. Indeed, the multitude of versions of *Antigone* produced from the sixteenth through to the present century, its fascination over and above virtually any other Greek tragedy for writers as diverse as Hegel and Hölderlin, Freud and Jung, Brecht and Anouilh, can be attributed largely to the fundamental dualities embodied in the play's characters. The problem, and the tragic source, in *Antigone* (as in each of the plays Kennelly has adapted) is that these opposites, however much they may reflect one another, remain irreconcilable.

Steiner contends that the excellence of Sophocles' play resides in its expression of the five major conflicts which govern the human condition. These he conveniently lists as: 'the confrontation of men and of women; of age and of youth; of society and of the individual; of the living and of the dead; of men and of god(s)', and goes on to analyse how, in their initial encounter, Antigone and Creon epitomise each category.[5] In opting to emphasise the dialectic of genders in his version, Kennelly has also chosen to highlight the drama's fundamental opposition. In doing so he is not, needless to say, breaking new ground. The subject of the play lends itself to a feminist interpretation, so it is not surprising that a number of feminist versions had appeared prior to 1984. But as Steiner is careful to note, it was not until the 1960s and the advent of 'women's liberation' that Antigone's radical feminism is championed over Ismene's generic conservatism. The prototype for subsequent stage productions in this vein was New York's Living Theatre interpretation for German audiences of Brecht's version of Hölderlin's translation, which instructs that 'Only women's authentic liberation, only the utter refusal of Ismene's *notre sexe imbécile*, will break the infernal circle...the false coupling of men and women in a traditional social order'.[6]

Kennelly adopts a comparable position in that, in his version of *Antigone*, the drama becomes a site of recovery where women are afforded expression of their 'unrestricted humanity', the male/female confrontation is centralised, and female rights, whether to despair, to connive, or to rage, are exposed as elemental to both the impact of the performance and to human nature. In constructing his play Kennelly was working out a clutch of immediate personal, cultural and aesthetic problems in a new medium and within the confines of a plot which, if he were to remain faithful to the original, denies the easy resolution of the conflicts and questions the play raises. In this respect the play is perhaps best understood as a 'workshop' where the groundwork for a developing dramaturgy and feminist aesthetic is hammered out.

The unique, double-edged love which is central to *Antigone* holds a special fascination for Kennelly:

> In *Antigone*... I wanted to explore sisterhood, the loyalty a sister will show to a brother, against law, against marriage, against everything. There's no relationship like it; it has all the passion of your whole nature, this side of incest...it was a study of a girl all of whose impulses defied everything, in order to bury the boy, to give him dignity.[7]

Antigone's devotion to her slain brother Polyneices is blood-begotten, unconditional. It transcends and therefore must defy the man-made laws of the city-state; it is the root cause of the antagonism between herself and Creon. But there is another sibling relationship whose contours are more problematic. If the play has become an emblematic feminist text, its status as such is in part due to the ramifications of the disagreement between Antigone and Ismene. Their initial exchange summarises the issue which informs the action and defines the two polarised responses to Creon's decree in Antigone's radical defiance and Ismene's conservative compliance. Although the immediate frame of reference is local and familial, the larger, non-specific subject of their debate is, in effect, the position of women in the governance of the city state and, by extension, the amount of actual control they are free to exercise over their own lives. Kennelly's diction makes it clear from the outset that Antigone and Ismene are bound by a common 'curse'. Not only the stigma attached to the house of Oedipus, a malaise which has brought them 'shame, dishonour, ruin, pain' and lately left them 'robbed of our two brothers', but their very womanhood, which renders them powerless to counter Creon's despotism, makes them doubly afflicted.

As the children of Oedipus, and as women, the sisters appear irrevocably fated. Yet Antigone and Ismene do not seem equally oppressed by their femininity. For Ismene being female means (perhaps as a matter of choice, certainly as a matter of course) being marginalised, uninformed. As her first words reveal:

> Antigone, not a single word of friends,
> Not a single happy or miserable word,
> Has reached me...
> I might as well be dead
> Because I know nothing more,
> Not, as I have said, one solitary word.

Whereas Ismene has been kept, or has kept herself, well back from the action, Antigone has been in the front lines, gathering information, weighing the meaning and the consequences of Creon's 'word'. Antigone's visit to Ismene is designed to test the latter's 'loyalty and love', to determine whether she is 'of noble blood' or simply 'the slavish slut/ Of a noble line'. If Antigone's words are hard, they are consonant with her attitude towards Ismene from the start. Her tone is reproachful of Ismene's isolation, and is reciprocated in Ismene's somewhat impatient description of Antigone as having been 'broody and wild' from childhood. Kennelly's diction connotes intellectual introspection, maternal anxiety and independent action, all characteristics Antigone possesses but which offend and inhibit Ismene's less assertive sensibility. Antigone has brought Ismene to a neutral zone, away from the male preserve of 'that court of sinister stone'. Here, the sisters are on 'female ground' and Ismene is free to think for herself. Her response to Antigone's challenge to help bury Polyneices, if not what she hopes for, is clearly what she expects. Ismene's assertion that they are 'mere women' who must not 'disobey the word of Creon' makes her position on the subordinate role of women, and therefore of Antigone's threat to upset that order, perfectly apparent. For Ismene, the authority of the state is paramount and she has neither the courage nor the conviction to go against it. Antigone, on the other hand, is not only unwilling but fundamentally unable to conform to the prescriptions of what she sees as an unjust law. Her loyalty is not to 'the ambitious living' but 'the mistreated, noble dead'. In choosing 'love' over 'frustration' she credits 'those laws/ Established in honour by the gods'. The law Antigone is talking about pre-dates and, in her view, transcends civil law: it is the law of kinship, which entails allegiance to a chthonic, intuitive, irrational but deeply religious sense of justice which is the inverse of Creon's rationalist meting of reward and punishment. Thus when Antigone speaks of her 'strength' as her most vital resource, what she means is the mental and spiritual conviction which keeps her sensitive to this knowledge. The case for civil disobedience as the 'right' reaction to self-aggrandising totalitarianism is virtually conceded in this opening exchange. Despite her departing reminder that 'Those who love you/ Will always hold you dear', the majority of modern productions impress that Ismene embodies the reactionary, visionless outlook of the status quo, in especial the sensible, even-minded women upon whom the state relies for its tacit support.

Kennelly's version is less single-minded in this respect. Without disturbing either the semantic richness or the political incisiveness of Sophocles, he manages to focus our attention first and foremost on the relationship between Antigone and Ismene as sisters and as women, and only secondarily on their function as the representatives of private and public interests, left- and right-wing thinking. We are made fully aware of the deep familial wounds which bind them, of their very different natures and, consequently, of the antagonisms which divide them. While he cannot but champion Antigone's heroic efforts, Kennelly is equally sympathetic to both sisters and is careful to emphasise that each is suppressed by Creon's strictures. he is at pains to draw out the tension between the sisters' love for one another and the difficulties they as women encounter in the political arena, and in turn to set that aspect of 'sisterhood' against Antigone's feelings about Polyneices. In seeking to define 'love', the question Kennelly asks is not which kind of love is greater – sister for sister, sister for brother – but how they are different, and what that difference tells us about human nature in general, and love in particular. He does this through a use of language which is direct and simple, yet emotive and poetically intricate. The dynamics of the sisters' relationship is conveyed through carefully modulated diction and intonation, which in turn directs us toward the issue of language and its centrality in the play.

Virginia Woolf was among the first feminist theorists to suggest that woman experience, think and therefore write the world differently from men.[8] The relevance of this proposition to Kennelly's

Antigone is worth pointing out: the exchange between Antigone and Ismene is essentially about correlations between language and gender, and so prepares us for Antigone's struggle towards 'articulate action'. Their debate is peppered with references to the power of language, from the initial allusion to the curse on the house of Oedipus through to Antigone's oath to make good her promise to bury her brother. The term 'word' is uttered no fewer than twenty times in the first 160 lines, and Kennelly's choice of repetition over variation is indicative of the weight he attaches to it.

While the play's primary conflict is between the power of authority invested in Creon's word and Antigone's bid to affirm that her promise is equally valid and right, the more subtle clash is between masculine and feminine discourse, between gendered ways of seeing and saying the world. Whereas Creon's language is the unequivocal and, as the chorus argues, necessarily uncompromising voice of effective government, the issue is complicated, and the drama enriched, by the fact that we are presented with at least two models of feminine discourse: Ismene's traditional posture of submissive silence and Antigone's vigorous challenge to patriarchy. The latter's 'cold words' are as rigid as Creon's, but with the difference that they involve the struggle for a language which fits her experience and her beliefs. Thus the question which becomes central to Kennelly's, as to any feminist, interpretation of the play is not simply which sister's stance is preferable, but which is in fact possible. The import of this opening section is succinctly summarised by Roche:

> The first scene between the sisters establishes a sense of woman not only taking over the moral vacuum left by men but transforming the image of heroism from violent self-assertiveness to ministering self-sacrifice.⁹

What follows is a development of this difference – the feminine alternative – via the enlargement of Kennelly's focus on gender and language. Each scene exposes the layers and ambiguities of the feminine incarnate in Antigone and her word made action.

Learning that someone has observed the rites he has outlawed, Creon is infuriated. In his ensuing tirade he twice reveals the unconscious assumption that such an act is beyond the province of any woman: 'What *man* alive would dare to do this thing?' and later, 'If you don't find the *man* who buried Polyneices/...You will be strung up alive' (*my emphasis*). The same dramatic irony informs the vocabulary of the chorus' second ode, beginning as it does with the celebrated lines 'Wonders are many/ And none is more wonderful than man'. Here too Kennelly exercises stark incremental repetition to underscore that, even as a candidate for the most marginalised of creatures, woman does not qualify in the popular imagination (again, the italics are mine here):

> Whoever dishonours the laws of the land,
> Scorns the justice loved by the gods,
> That *man* has no city,
> That *man* must live where no one lives.
> Never may he visit my home,
> Never share my thoughts.
> That *man* must know his madness is his own
> And is not part of the people.
> *He* is a severed limb,
> A severed head
> Unacceptable to the conscious living
> And the restful dead.

The impact of the guard's revelation that Antigone, a 'mere girl', is the malefactor leaves the chorus stunned, Creon 'doubly-insulted'. The avian imagery which studs his report of her discovery sets Creon's curses 'Beating like the wings of maddened birds/ About to swoop and rip my brains and heart out' against Antigone's maternal rage. Whereas Creon's threats carry the weight of imminent punishment, Antigone's pain renders her all but inarticulate, grasping for another means of pronouncing her sorrow:

> I saw this girl. She gave a sharp cry
> Like a wounded bird or a mother
> Brutally stripped of her children.
> When she saw the corpse deprived
> Of the covering dignity of dust,
> She cried a cry beyond all bounds of words
> And cursed whoever did that deed.

The association of pathetic fallacy with Antigone's retreat from language is followed by a crucial exchange in which Creon addresses her in blatantly sexist terms. However, her immediate, subversive response marks a recovery of language and a recognition that she must learn to use it in her own way and to achieve her own ends:

> CREON. You, *girl*, staring at the earth,
>   Do you admit, or do you deny,
>   This deed?
> ANTIGONE. (*Looking up.*) I admit it, *man*.

Antigone's challenge to Creon's masculine ethos is double-edged. When she asserts 'Word and deed are one in me./ That is my glory' and goes on to disclose that the people in fact support her but are silent in fear of Creon's reaction, she threatens not just to undermine the basis of his authority and power, but to equal and possibly surpass his perceived sexual superiority as well. In short, Antigone implies that she will live as a man, something Creon fails to tolerate or understand: 'I would be no man,/ She would be the man/ If I let her go unpunished'.

In aligning herself with the non-secular otherworld of the gods, the underworld of the dead, Antigone seeks to counter hatred with love, to reinstate the non-patriarchal, alternative values of blood and family in place of the interventionist laws of the city-state. So complete is her commitment that she has chosen martyrdom over betrayal. As she reminds Ismene, 'I chose to die for love', 'My life is an act of service to the dead'. Yet however independent, her defiance is also an arguably self-interested gesture. For in her admonition of Ismene – 'There were two worlds, two ways./ One world approved your way,/ The other, mine' – and later the chorus – 'You know all about men...power...money...But you know nothing of women' – Antigone reveals what amounts to a personal religion which is prototypically feminist in premise and mode. For while she may oppose Creon on his own ground, 'as a man', she does not renounce her femininity; on the contrary, she pushes ever more deeply into that paradoxically new yet familiar territory where identity and sexuality are coterminous. Indeed, so unique is her venture that it carries her beyond the experience of either sex: 'I am a woman without fear/ In a hole in the rocks/ Where no man or woman dare venture'. Yet as a woman, Antigone is unaccustomed to such control and responsibility, and the prospect of self-creation is frightening, something which would choke her 'like a chicken-bone/ Stuck in my throat...Like ivy choking a house'. Trepidation, however, rapidly reverts to conviction, so much so that she can make the quasi-hubristic claim 'If I lived,/ I could change all the men of the world'.

The magnitude of the individual and the institution she is up against is fully exposed in Creon's treatment of Antigone and Ismene, and in particular of his own son, Haemon. His 'advice' to Haemon quickly degenerates into a diatribe in which women like Antigone are denounced as 'treacherous' and 'disobedient', and sons instructed not to think for themselves but 'Obey [their] father's will in everything'. This oration is symptomatic of his fear of being shamed by a woman – 'If I must fall from power/ Let it be by a man's hand,/ Never by a woman's'. Haemon's temperate appeal for a more democratic, pluralist, feminised form of government meets with a predictable rebuke: 'You would put a man below a woman...

Go be a woman/ Since you understand the thing so well'. We are returned to Antigone's words to the chorus which, in the light of Haemon's predicament, remind us of the difficulties involved in making a place for women in established male centred codes:

What man
Knows anything of women?

If he did
He would change from being a man
As men recognise a man.

Finally imprisoned in 'the loneliest place in the world...a hole among the rocks', Antigone has made, it seems, the highest sacrifice, exchanging marriage and children for a tomb.

The physical immediacy of her oblation links her 'body language' to accepted notions about the necessarily corporeal, non-literate nature of female creativity and self-expression, as well as bringing it into line with the intuitive, emotive sphere she represents. By the same token, however, it identifies female creativity – Antigone's 'word' – solely with female sexuality. Her individual protest is ironically overcome by her gender, and the gap between male and female remains unbridgeable. To see Antigone's tragic victory in this way is to concede that because she is a 'mere woman' she cannot, nor should she ever presume to, achieve the autonomy she seeks, or address Creon in a language which is 'sexually pluralist' and therefore politically effective.

Antigone's solitary courage *does* make her an exemplary woman ahead of her time, but the 'body language' she uses to state her case, and to achieve what measure of revenge she can, is in fact a non-language. The audience is made to question the masculine hierarchy Creon stands for, but at the price of Antigone's silence. 'If I lived I would change all men.' *If* she lived. Within the parameters of the play, however, her declamatory gesture dies with her and she remains a victim, compelled in her death to share the silence Ismene recommends in the opening scene. Where Antigone's language survives, of course, is in each new performance of the play.

I suggested earlier that Kennelly's *Antigone* is a 'workshop' for both his move towards writing for the stage and the development of a feminist aesthetic. In terms of imagery, diction and characterisation, it is obviously connected to his poetry; in terms of issues and concerns it strikes out more forcefully than he had previously done at the oppressive forces of patriarchy in contemporary, particularly Irish, society in the seventies and eighties. As Kennelly shapes it, *Antigone* becomes a cautionary tale of sorts, warning both the Creons and the Antigones (whether we understand them in socio-political or psycho-sexual terms) in his audiences against the dangers, in the first instance, of denying the feminine, and in the second, of 'excessive love', of making 'too great a sacrifice' and an end in silence. Kennelly's *Antigone is* a play for and about women. Not only does it give Irish women a voice familiar in idiom and interest, but alongside caution it offers encouragement, finding in Antigone a model for the strength and conviction required to be 'mistress of your own fate', the author of your own language. The black hole Antigone must descend into is on one level an emblem of annihilating silence. But on another it represents the next stage on the journey towards 'articulate action' which is the destiny of all the Antigones we encounter in Kennelly's writing. Without that descent we would not have the voices of Medea and Hecuba and Cassandra or Lorca's Spanish wives and widows, for it is in this darkness that Kennelly has listened most intently to women as they learn to rage.

Extract from Kathleen McCracken's essay 'Rage for a New Order: Brendan Kennelly's Plays for Women', in *Dark Fathers into Light: Brendan Kennelly*, edited by Richard Pine (Bloodaxe Books, 1994).

NOTES:
1. George Steiner, *Antigones* (Oxford: Clarendon Press, 1984), p.138.
2. Anthony Roche, 'Ireland's *Antigones*: Tragedy North and South', *Cultural Contexts and Literary Idioms in Contemporary Irish Literature*, edited by Michael Kenneally (Gerrards Cross: Colin Smythe, 1988), pp.221-50.
3. Roche, p.246.
4. Kennelly, 'Learning From Our Contradictions', *Ireland: Look, The Land Is Bright* (Ireland Funds Conference Proceedings, 1990), p.23.
5. Steiner, p.231 ff.
6. Steiner, p.150.
7. Kennelly, 'Q. & A. with Brendan Kennelly', with Richard Pine, *Irish Literary Supplement*, 9.1 (Spring 1991), p.22.
8. Virginia Woolf, *A Room of One's Own* (1929; New York: Harcourt, Brace, Jovanovich, 1981), pp.97-104.
9. Roche, p.242.

WRITERS PUBLISHED BY
BLOODAXE BOOKS

FLEUR ADCOCK
GÖSTA ÅGREN
ANNA AKHMATOVA
GILLIAN ALLNUTT
SIMON ARMITAGE
NEIL ASTLEY
ANNEMARIE AUSTIN
JOSEPHINE BALMER
ELIZABETH BARTLETT
MARTIN BELL
CONNIE BENSLEY
STEPHEN BERG
SARA BERKELEY
JAMES BERRY
ATTILIO BERTOLUCCI
YVES BONNEFOY
KARIN BOYE
KAMAU BRATHWAITE
BEVERLIEY BRAUNE
ELEANOR BROWN
BASIL BUNTING
RON BUTLIN
CIARAN CARSON
JOHN CASSIDY
AIMÉ CÉSAIRE
SID CHAPLIN
RENÉ CHAR
GEORGE CHARLTON
EILÉAN NÍ CHUILLEANÁIN
KILLARNEY CLARY
BRENDAN CLEARY
JACK CLEMO
HARRY CLIFTON
JACK COMMON
STEWART CONN
DAVID CONSTANTINE
JANE COOPER
JULIA COPUS
JENI COUZYN
FRED D'AGUIAR
PETER DIDSBURY
STEPHEN DOBYNS
MAURA DOOLEY
KATIE DONOVAN
FREDA DOWNIE
JOHN DREW
IAN DUHIG
HELEN DUNMORE
JACQUES DUPIN
G.F. DUTTON
LAURIS EDMOND
MENNA ELFYN
ALISTAIR ELLIOT
STEVE ELLIS
PAUL ÉLUARD
ODYSSEUS ELYTIS
HANS MAGNUS
ENZENSBERGER
EURIPIDES
DAVID FERRY
EVA FIGES
SYLVA FISCHEROVÁ

ROY FISHER
TONY FLYNN
CAROLYN FORCHÉ
VICTORIA FORDE
TUA FORSSTRÖM
LINDA FRANCE
ANDRÉ FRÉNAUD
TESS GALLAGHER
ELIZABETH GARRETT
PAMELA GILLILAN
ANDREW GREIG
CHRIS GREENHALGH
JOHN GREENING
PHILIP GROSS
MAGGIE HANNAN
JOSEF HANZLÍK
TONY HARRISON
GEOFF HATTERSLEY
ADRIAN HENRI
TRACEY HERD
W.N. HERBERT
MIGUEL HERNÁNDEZ
HAROLD HESLOP
DOROTHY HEWETT
RITA ANN HIGGINS
SELIMA HILL
FRIEDRICH HÖLDERLIN
MIROSLAV HOLUB
FRANCES HOROVITZ
DOUGLAS HOUSTON
JOHN HUGHES
PAUL HYLAND
PHILIPPE JACCOTTET
KATHLEEN JAMIE
VLADIMÍR JANOVIC
LINTON KWESI JOHNSON
JOOLZ
JENNY JOSEPH
SYLVIA KANTARIS
JACKIE KAY
BRENDAN KENNELLY
HELEN KITSON
STEPHEN KNIGHT
JEAN HANFF KORELITZ
DENISE LEVERTOV
GWYNETH LEWIS
MARION LOMAX
EDNA LONGLEY
FEDERICO GARCÍA LORCA
PETER McDONALD
MEDBH McGUCKIAN
MAIRI MacINNES
CHRISTINE McNEILL
OSIP MANDELSTAM
GERALD MANGAN
E.A. MARKHAM
DON MARQUIS
WILLIAM MARTIN
GLYN MAXWELL
PAULA MEEHAN
HENRI MICHAUX
ADRIAN MITCHELL

JOHN MONTAGUE
EUGENIO MONTALE
DAVID MORLEY
RICHARD MURPHY
BILL NAUGHTON
HENRY NORMAL
SEAN O'BRIEN
JULIE O'CALLAGHAN
DOUGLAS OLIVER
OTTÓ ORBÁN
MICHEAL O'SIADHAIL
RUTH PADEL
GYÖRGY PETRI
TOM PICKARD
JILL PIRRIE
KATRINA PORTEOUS
TOM POW
SIMON RAE
DEBORAH RANDALL
IRINA RATUSHINSKAYA
MARIA RAZUMOVSKY
PETER READING
PETER REDGROVE
DERYN REES-JONES
ANNE ROUSE
CAROL RUMENS
LAWRENCE SAIL
ANN SANSOM
PETER SANSOM
SAPPHO
DAVID SCOTT
OLIVE SENIOR
JO SHAPCOTT
ELENA SHVARTS
MATT SIMPSON
DAVE SMITH
KEN SMITH
STEPHEN SMITH
EDITH SÖDERGRAN
PIOTR SOMMER
SOPHOCLES
MARIN SORESCU
LEOPOLD STAFF
PAULINE STAINER
EIRA STENBERG
MARTIN STOKES
RABINDRANATH TAGORE
JEAN TARDIEU
D.M. THOMAS
R.S. THOMAS
TOMAS TRANSTRÖMER
MARINA TSVETAYEVA
MIRJAM TUOMINEN
LILIANA URSU
MIROSLAV VÁLEK
PAUL VALÉRY
FRED VOSS
NIGEL WELLS
C.K. WILLIAMS
JOHN HARTLEY WILLIAMS
JAMES WRIGHT
BENJAMIN ZEPHANIAH

For a complete catalogue of books published by Bloodaxe, please write to:
Bloodaxe Books Ltd, P.O. Box 1SN, Newcastle upon Tyne NE99 1SN.